the joy of
doing
        just
enough

Also by Jennifer McCartney

The Joy of Leaving Your Sh*t All Over the Place

Poetry from Scratch

Cocktails for Drinkers

Afloat

the joy of
doing
just
enough

the secret art of being lazy and getting away with it

jennifer mccartney

the countryman press
a division of w. w. norton & company
independent publishers since 1923

For information about permission to reproduce selections
from this book, write to Permissions, The Countryman Press,
500 Fifth Avenue, New York, NY 10110

For information about special discounts for bulk purchases,
please contact W. W. Norton Special Sales at
specialsales@wwnorton.com or 800-233-4830

Manufacturing by QuadGraphics, Fairfield
Book design by Nick Caruso Design
Production manager: Devon Zahn

The Countryman Press
www.countrymanpress.com

A division of W. W. Norton & Company, Inc.
500 Fifth Avenue, New York, NY 10110
www.wwnorton.com

978-1-68268-146-6

10 9 8 7 6 5 4 3 2 1

author's note

I have a secret to tell you. You are not lazy. You are not a failure. You are not unproductive. The idea that we need to be constantly productive and operating at 100 percent is just some capitalist bullshit we've been conditioned to believe in by society. Unless you live in France, of course, where the government gives you five months of vacation and you get paid in cases of Syrah.

This book is for those of you who need to let it all go and practice the art of doing just enough.

contents

I don't fetch

THE TOP TEN THINGS
JUST-ENOUGH PEOPLE KNOW

....

"I'm lazy. But it's the lazy people who invented the wheel and the bicycle because they didn't like walking or carrying things."
—LECH WALESA

1. Anything can be a spoon

2. Deadlines are a suggestion

3. As are best-before dates

4. OJ works in cereal if you're out of milk

5. Life is too short

6. All your furniture should have a remote control: La-Z-Boy, liquor cabinet, mattress

7. Lists are for suckers

8. 10 things is too many things

Introduction

n: *satisficiency* def: *the art of doing just enough to satisfy everyone*

We're not conditioned to do just enough. We're supposed to always be prepared, and be early, and always deliver more than we promised. You're supposed to hustle. Get ahead. Outperform your peers. Get the promotion, the good grades, the scholarship. Being average isn't what we're brought up to value. A 2014 study from Harvard shows that out of 10,000 middle and high school students almost half said that "achieving at a high level" was more important than happiness or caring for others. What the fuck, society? Trust me kids, no one will ever give a fuck about your 95 percent in grade eleven biology if you also pushed someone down the stairs to get to class on time.

So what would it take for you to do just enough—to just be getting by? Maybe you're already there! Maybe you're already doing just barely enough to get by, but have been conditioned to think that it's not enough. You're alive. But it's not enough! You should be succeeding more! You should be overachieving! Exhausting thought, right? The key to life is doing just enough. Do what's expected of you, most of the time. This allows you to accept that your current output is enough, but it also allows you to appear productive and to function in a society that just doesn't get why the constant struggle to be better is actually damaging us.

The three key takeaways from this book:

1. Lazy* people live longer.

2. Lazy people work better and more efficiently.

3. Numbered lists are bullshit.

In spite of the pressure from society to plan ahead and overachieve, I've discovered that the just-enough method is the best way to get things

* Don't let the lazy label fool you. It's time to take back the word. Just like "messiness" is actually associated with creativity and a willingness to try new things, laziness has its benefits. Allow yourself some space to relax, and what you worried was laziness is actually the best way to get shit done.

done. Fuck your to-do lists, schedules, flow-charts, group chats, conference calls, and general readiness. It doesn't work for everyone, and the expectation to be great, or to be better, or to strive for improvement, or qualify for a promotion, or to arrive prepared, is stressful. And unrealistic, for most of us—those of us just trying to get by. Anyone who's ever left the house late for an appointment with a cell phone battery at 8 percent and cat hair on their pants will understand.

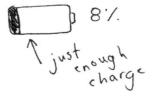

The key to success isn't working too hard; it's working just hard enough—never overpromising, never overachieving. So keep reading. I can show you how to quit your striving and settle for doing just enough. I can show you the FIB method to successfully chilling the fuck out.

Reset your life by vowing never to do more than you have to

Forget about success and strive for satisficiency. Don't worry about spelling it. Read this and realize the secret to doing just enough. Read this and fall asleep. Read this and write a think piece about how doing just enough is the new unicorn latte. First, you need to learn the essential three steps to doing just enough, because everyone knows that improvement requires a set of instructions that can easily be reproduced on a throw pillow.

unicorn latte.

Fuck your mantras

Why you're not a badass and that's okay. You also don't need to "unfuck yourself" or learn the art of not giving a fuck.

fuck mantras

Mantras used to be just for yoga retreats and meditation and trust falls ("don't fucking drop me" is a mantra) but they're popular in the corporate and self-help world, too. "Mantra" is Sanskrit for "sacred thought" or "sacred utterance." Businesses love these sacred thoughts: "be generous and brave" at your gray cubicle. Suffer "no bullshit" in your nap pod in Silicon Valley. "Be relentless" while writing code for an insurance company. If you work at Google, just "don't be evil." Whichever one appeals to you it's time to cut that shit out. Talking to yourself (also called "self-affirmations") is not the key to success.

You know what one of the top search terms is when you look for instructions on "how to be a badass?" "How to look like a badass when you're short." Yeah. So, just forget it. You're really not going to change your personality. Or your height. Yet being a badass is one of the numerous new self-help attitudes we've been asked to embrace of late.

shit kickers

Put on your shit-kickers and stare down the patriarchy. While also being grateful for the vitality and energy that allows you to kick so much life in the ass. While we're at it, fuck feelings, too. And please do this self-improvement in between your two jobs and after you run to the bathroom to get some soap and water on this avocado stain. And maybe also after you've finished walking your dad through the new features on his cell phone. And after you help your daughter make dragon-scale slime for show and tell tomorrow. Who has the time?

Look, very few people in this world are actual badasses: Wonder Woman. The Mafia. Sloths. Representative John Lewis. Trying to be a badass and celebrating the art of being a badass is the least badass thing I've ever heard of. So cut that shit out. It's just another way of making you feel like you should be a different way from how you are.

I get that it feels empowering for a few minutes to read a book that tells you how to be really cool. "I'm going to be cool now," you might think, after finishing a book like that. I've definitely just unfucked myself, you'll think excitedly. But trying to achieve a kind of blasé coolness is the same kind of prescriptive bullshit that told you to find joy in your belongings and a clean house. Oh, look at me being a badass, you might think, after deleting an email or closing all the tabs on your browser or adding whole milk to your cereal. Trying to be cool wasn't cool when you were 12. It's not going to work for you now.

THE SECOND STEP:
Indifference is essential

Being successful is a big fucking deal in our society. It's measured in a myriad of ways including:

- Making a lot of money.

- Having millions of social media followers.

- Having photogenic, healthy children.

- Having a six-pack or a hot post-baby body.

- Owning and decorating a piece of real estate in such a trendy way that it's then featured on Apartment Therapy. Usually this involves cacti (real and in paintings), brass or copper finishes in your bedroom, bathroom, or kitchen, and lots of white paint.

cactus

- Having a trendy, expensive dog (looking at you, labradoodles).

- Owning a boat.

- Having well-proportioned toes that photograph well in sandals (i.e., not finger toes).

- Being employed somewhere with good name recognition: Google, *The New York Times*, Tesla, Margaritaville, NASA, etc.

labrado·dle

- How often you cancel plans because you're just "overwhelmed." This is impressive for a while because it makes you seem very important. But soon your friends will think you're an asshole and start saying snotty things like, "What the fuck. It's not like they're trying to make partner at a law firm. They work in marketing for Sears."

Wanting to have these things and not having them can be the source of much frustration. You're not successful and you do not appear successful to your friends and family. This is where indifference is key. You need to opt out of the wanting. You need to be indifferent to society's measures of success. This isn't a trick where now I tell you that once you have become indifferent, THAT'S when success will hit. It won't. But you will no longer care. So, whatever. Nice yacht, I guess.

this is how
I draw a
yacht

satisficieny tip

If you still want to appear successful to strangers,
I suggest expensive business cards that say
"entrepreneur," "writer," or "producer." People will
suspect it's bullshit, but they won't know for sure.
Once my friend was on a date and she asked
what the guy did for a living. "I go where the money
goes," was what he told her.
This is the equivalent of a business card that says
"businessperson." He's giving the appearance
of success, and you might as well believe him until
you discover that he's unemployed (which is what
happened with my friend and her date).

THE THIRD STEP:
Being busy is bullshit

Mantras can be useful as long as they aren't lame. So learn this one: Being busy is bullsit. Learning this cool mantra doesn't cancel out step one, so don't @ me. We glorify the art of busyness. It's a sickness. We're afraid of being idle. Of being alone with our thoughts. Of not having enough to do or enough to show for our time on this earth. So we worship at the altar of doing stuff. But you know what? Being busy is for idiots.

Studies show the smarter you are, the lazier you tend to be. How does that work? People with a high IQ can sit around and be perfectly content with their own thoughts. No activity required. This is a great fact to tell your parents when they ask about why you lie around all day. Repeat after me: Being busy is bullshit.

Fit to be FIB

Now that you've mastered steps one through three, you're what we call an FIB expert. Fuck your mantras. Indifference is essential. Being busy is bullshit. When you put these steps together they spell FIB. Fibbing is the key to doing just enough. You got it? You're learning it's okay to just get by. In fact, it's better than okay. It's a relief and you're a lot happier now, right? People like that about you. Your just-enough attitude isn't intimidating. It makes you approachable. People want to be your friend. And you know what? You've got time for friends now that you're not working late at your job.

ponder the clouds

turtles are your friends

fuck your mantras
Indifference is key
being busy is bullshit

practice your eye roll

TO
DO
1. chill

1.

Just Enough at Home

*"If you just feel lazy and don't want to cook,
then don't cook."*

—TOM DOUGLAS

Keeping a clean and organized household is something some people do. I'm assuming those people aren't the kinds of people who pick up a book like this.

So, here's to all of us who struggle to remember to take out the garbage and who don't have marble countertops and cleaning ladies and gold bathroom fixtures and alphabetized pantries. Here's to those of us with a rented apartment and linoleum floors and wire coat hangers and a fridge full of cheese.

The just-enough method is here to help you sort out the requirements of life (eating) from the bullshit (taking a photo of what you're eating).

COOKING:

Where frozen foods and takeout rule, fuck that Blue Apron shit

"The quest for slowness, which begins as a simple rebellion against the impoverishment of taste in our lives, makes it possible to rediscover taste."

—CARLO PETRINI[*]

This quote is fine if you like things that take forever, like home-cooked meals. Luckily for us, science has invented ways to eat faster. Thanks, microwaves!

Our brilliant ancestors invented frozen and canned foods (mostly so the military could do war better) and the results were glorious. These prepackaged foods presented our mothers and grandmothers with a convenient way to feed their families without a lot of hassle. It was the height of the just-enough era. By all accounts, my English grandmother used to eat mushy peas

---

[*] Founder of the international Slow Food movement

from a tin while smoking Benson & Hedges and entertaining her numerous male visitors. Easy. It used to be the latest fashion to have a stocked pantry full of delicious tins of tuna and peas. Dinner parties were all about Jell-O desserts filled with mandarin oranges from a can. Hurrah for progress and the gradual liberation of women from the kitchen, they probably thought. Except that's not what happened. We're as chained to expectations of culinary prowess as we have ever been.

Today, dining on canned and frozen foods is frowned upon. We're not supposed to eat cereal at midnight or a peanut butter sandwich for breakfast. When it comes to the kitchen, we're no longer allowed to do just enough. We're supposed to serve organic, dairy-free, probiotic, whole-grain milk and kale grown on your rooftop garden. The convenience of prepackaged food is outweighed by our snobbery and our wariness about it. Is the metal in the can leaching toxins into your food? Is it canned in water or oil? Is it BPA-free? Is it organic? Is it from the local market? Were you acquainted with this pig before it became your bacon? Did you make it yourself?

Now we've come full circle, where meal delivery services send you all your food uncooked, uncanned, and unfrozen. And you have to cook it. That's not fucking progress. We've gone from cold food pre-packed in our freezers and hot takeout delivered to our door to uncooked meal delivery kits. Why do I want something delivered to my house that I have to cook? That's adding an extra step of bullshit.

When it comes to cooking, there should only be one real measure of success. Are you full? Is your family full? Good. Lucky for you.

satisficieny tip

Add some spring onions to your can of chili. Add grated Cheddar to that frozen burrito. Add some blueberries to your cereal. It's just enough.

"The kitchen oven is reliable, but it's made us lazy."

—JAMIE OLIVER[*]

THE TOP FIVE
TIME SAVING-KITCHEN TRICKS

....

1. Boil some water at the beginning of the week and freeze it in single-portion containers. That way you'll have it on hand when you need it for cooking.

2. Put the head of lettuce you picked up on your recent shopping trip directly into the garbage. Saves you throwing it away next week.

3. Microwave it. 30 seconds on high. Done.

....

[*] Talking shit about an appliance that lets us heat stuff up without having to actually start a fire first

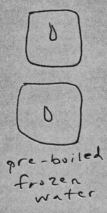

pre-boiled
frozen
water

4. Don't grow your own herbs. They immediately turn brown or white and then you feel like a failure. No one eats that much fresh basil anyway.

5. Ugh. Lists. Four things is enough.

The pressure to make beautiful food

In addition to the societal pressure to cook fresh-from-the-garden meals, we're also expected to make our meals look stylish. Charcoal ice cream, matcha-crusted salmon, anything on toast. Then you're supposed to Instagram it.

Have you ever tried to take a picture of your food? It's going to look like shit. It's going to look washed out or yellow or lumpy no matter what filter you use. I once waited an hour for a coffee ice cream thing in Chicago. The idea was that the ice cream came with a donut impaled on a red swirly straw and that it looked really cool. I happily took forty photos of it (in front of a brick wall, in front of a plant, in front of the dessert store's hipster sign) and they all looked like shit. Blurry, dark, and unappetizing. And that's cool. I'm not a fucking photography expert and my phone takes pictures that look like it's been bathed in Vaseline so whatever. I ate it and no one will ever know how pretty it looked in real life.

But the pressure to make our own food look like an art installation is fierce. We're supposed to make beautiful acai bowls with rainbow colors (acai, kiwi, mango, strawberry, arranged in an arc) that you can then Instagram. You're supposed to make your kid's hummus sandwich look like a dinosaur or a manga character. Then you're supposed to post it so people can say things like, "Where do you find the time?!" Forget it. And eat your fucking food.

● satisficieny ●
tip

Ditch the cell phone.

are you a just-enough gourmet?

1. When it comes to making dinner your strategy is:

    A. Chicken breast, some baby carrots, and I dunno, some lime juice? Rice? Whatever.

    B. I ordered Thai online on my way home. Should be there when I arrive.

    C. Whole grain bowl with farro, feta, mango, dried seaweed, and a pomegranate aril garnish.

2. Your idea of fine dining is:

    A. Adding bacon bits to the potato salad.

    B. Microwaving the leftover sushi. Who likes fish cold, anyway?

    C. Champagne-marinated caviar followed by poached King salmon and salted radishes.

3. When you realize the Cheddar has been left on the counter for a few hours you:

   A. Make a grilled cheese with some leftover hamburger buns.

   B. Cut off another slice.

   C. Oh, we don't eat Cheddar in my house. We prefer soft, French cheeses.

Answer Key:

Mostly As: Nice work. You cooked food, albeit in a minimal half-assed way, and will still have time to watch a show.

Mostly Bs: The joy of doing just enough. Feels great, doesn't it?

Mostly Cs: Everyone at your baby playgroup hates you.

← eat it. You'll be dead soon anyway

HOUSEKEEPING:
The messier things get, the more doing the minimum satisfies

"I hate housework! You make the beds, you do the dishes and six months later you have to start all over again."

—JOAN RIVERS

Society expects a clean house. Then, when you do keep a clean house or bedroom or apartment, people come to expect it from you. Those expectations pile up and stress you out. But you have to keep on keeping shit tidy because it's your job. It's what we original writers who love language like to call a "vicious cycle."

Anyway, as you already know, keeping your environment clean and tidy isn't sustainable. Inevitably something in your life happens and you can't be the overachieving clean person. Instead you're the "holy shit s/he's really let things go I'm worried about them" person. Stop cleaning your room and your parents will suspect you're smoking a lot of weed and shoplifting eye-liners from the local drugstore. Stop trimming the hedges and let your gutters fill with leaves every fall* and your next-door neighbor will start eying your recycling bin full of wine bottles and gossiping about how you can't handle mother-hood after all. Never let the benchmark get that high. You want to be neat enough that no one remarks on your dirty house and untidy enough that when everything goes to shit it's very hard to tell. This is called the neat/sloppy method.

● satisficieny ●
tip

Buy one of those magic erasers.
Wipe all the scuff marks off of your paint and
chair and table legs and floor. Bask in the glory
of a photo-shoot-ready living space.

....

* You know what happens when you do that shit? Come win-ter, snow melts into the stopped-up gutters and then over-flows and refreezes and you have big amazing icicles hanging down from the eaves that your kids can break off and play with. Most likely they won't fall and impale you or them.

41

CLEANING:
Killing just enough germs to keep your immune system healthy

When I was little, my mother let me play in mud puddles. I remember this because a neighbor saw me in the street one day and was upset. My mother, who grew up in a cornfield in Iowa, was of the "your kid survived childbirth so it can survive anything" generation. She didn't give a shit about dirt and told the neighbor so, but in a very nice way because she was also Canadian. I probably learned to wash my hands somewhere, I guess. But overall I embraced dirt, and to this day there's not much that grosses me out. Warm subway poles, for example. Hot from the hands of my fellow man. Whatever!

This attitude is backed up by science: You already know that antibacterial soap is bad for you. It kills off microbes that actually strengthen your immune system. So rather than killing germs, we should be letting them do their thing.

The right bacteria can mean fewer allergies, digestion issues, and a whole shitload of time saved by not obsessing over cleaning everything.

But we're still buying thousands of cleaning products and wiping everything down with expensive sponges designed to murder bacteria. First it was just obvious stuff you had to decontaminate like bathtubs and kitchen counters. Then our phone screens. Our doorknobs. I just saw an ad for shoes you can wash because the soles of our shoes collect grime and bacteria. I'm here to tell you: Stop bleaching your toothbrush every fortnight and get healthy by doing less. The more cleaning you do, the more antibacterial soaps and wipes you use, the worse it is for your

immune system. Another case of going overboard when doing just enough would suffice.

• satisficieny •
tip

Clean your kitchens and bathrooms the way our grandmothers did: some vinegar and hot water and a little prayer and forget it. Unless you're licking toilet seats, you'll be just fine. And healthy.

WE HAVE TO WORRY ABOUT OUR FUCKING FRUIT NOW?

....

Cleaning fresh fruit properly is now a thing. There are now special fruit washes you can buy that promise to remove all the bacteria from your apples and kumquats. Washing fruit with water only removes about 85 percent of bacteria according to studies. Does anyone give a shit about the remaining 15 percent? Do you know of anyone who has actually died from eating a germy apple? Just do the bare minimum and run that shit underwater, but otherwise, please worry about getting hit by a bus. Damage from that is more likely than from apple germs your body will fight off anyway.

satisficieny tip

When someone asks if the apple is washed, say yes. You're doing them a favor.

PETS:
Feed and water them and ditch the expensive dog shampoo

Pets want you around a lot. They also want to be fed regularly. They don't really need expensive grooming, organic food, fancy clothing, and a Harvard-educated behavioral psychologist to take them for a walk. (I could say the same about kids, actually.)

Obviously there's a reason people are very into their pets. They're relaxing to look at. When they're all curled up, they look like little croissants. They are very loving. If they're cats, they smell fine at all times (sorry dogs). I'm not super into dogs, except for the medium-sized ones that have floppy ears—big enough to look like a proper dog, small enough that I'm not worried about my throat getting ripped out if I look at it wrong. Anyway. People go overboard with their pets and dress them up and spend tons of money on them and enter them into contests. They also like to brag about the breed. Oh, she's a ragdoll, they'll say. Feel free to follow her on our social media channels! All my cats were rescue cats, so I don't really get the obsession with having an expensive pet as a status symbol. The point is, owning a pet should be mostly about loving that pet. Not about what that pet says about you and your success.

satisficieny
tip

Remember to feed your pets. Pet them when you remember. Take them with you if you have to evacuate. Look, just love them all the time, okay? The rest of life is hard and shitty, but your pets are a bright spot.

Quiz

what kind of cat are you?

1. When your boss appears at your office door to ask why you haven't replied to the email she sent four minutes ago do you:

  A. Look up at her sleepily, blink your eyes a few times, and turn back to your computer screen.

  B. Look up suddenly, sweep a bunch of things off your desk, and then bolt from the room.

  C. Calmly tell your boss you're putting out a few fires and will get to her email shortly.

  D. Say, "Oh I'm so glad you're here! You always brighten my day!

2. When you're at a dinner party you:

  A. Sit regally in a corner chair, surveying the room, speaking to no one like a complete asshole.

  B. Follow the host around the kitchen, staring at the roast chicken. Ask when the food is going to be ready a lot.

C. Pat yourself on the back for showing up to a dinner party.

D. Dole out small amounts of attention to various dinner guests, then make a quick exit back home to your couch/pajamas.

Answer Key

Mostly As: Too much cat, honestly, you're going to get fired and lose all your friends. There's a reason there are no cat CEOs. Or any cat with a job ever. You're one of those standoffish cats nobody except their owners likes.

Mostly Bs: See a. You're a maniac cat. You make people uncomfortable. Behind your back, people are wondering if you're on drugs. You're the reason dog-people don't like cats.

Mostly Cs: You're a cool person. Not very cat-like, but you'll probably get by in life without freaking out too much.

Mostly Ds: Excellent cat behavior. You can give and take affection with the best of them. You keep people off balance just enough that they're uncomfortable. You are just enough cat.

2.

Just Enough at Work

"Most people work just hard enough not to get fired and get paid just enough money not to quit."

—GEORGE CARLIN

We've all been encouraged to work hard to achieve success. To want (and get) promotions. To rise to the top. To be the best!

We associate success with working late, coming in early, overachieving, and never taking too many sick days or vacation days. The Society for Human Resource Management found that 70 percent of employees surveyed worked late and worked on weekends. Why? "Self-imposed pressure," was the response.

It isn't really self-imposed though, you poor overworked assholes. It's society. And it's fucking you over. The just-enough method is here to help.

OFFICE:
Working less means better work

"Ambition is a poor excuse for not having
sense enough to be lazy."
—MILAN KUNDERA

I used to work with a woman who proudly told me she hadn't used any of her vacation days that year. Obviously, she sucked on a personal level and fucked up a lot at work because she worked too hard, but everyone gave her a pass because she worked so hard and so late, all the time. The problem is that she wasn't working efficiently. She was overworking to the point of being a liability, and also she was incredibly boring to talk to because she had no social life outside of work. She burned out shortly thereafter and probably runs a yoga retreat now.

You know what works better than working all the time? Not working all the time, according to a study outlined in the Harvard Business

Review. A group of consulting teams at a Boston company were instructed to take a scheduled break during the workday. They also weren't allowed to work late or on weekends. The result? Communication, planning, and office relationships improved and so did client satisfaction.

The point of all this is to say: You're working too hard. You need to work less. You need to work enough. Enough to keep both your job and your sanity. Easy.

satisficieny
tip

Go home.

CUBICLE:
Looking busy is enough

"I'm barely prolific and incredibly lazy."
—TOM PETTY

Looking busy at work is important, unfortunately—more important than the work you actually do. A study by the Modern Nomad found 51 percent of millennials across the globe admit to faking their level of busyness. No shit.

I worked with a guy once who'd sigh and look concerned whenever you asked him to do something. He'd gesture to a pile of whatever on his desk and be like, "I can try, but . . ." Then he'd shake his head and kind of chuckle like, "Gosh, what a lot of work I'm required to do each day." This act was designed to demonstrate how he was too busy for your bullshit and how sorry he was about it. Eventually you'd get irritated and stop asking him to do anything.

My boss loved him because my boss assumed this employee was very fucking busy all the time when I know for a fact he was updating his band's website and taking two-hour lunch breaks at the pub down the street. It should have been a lesson for me. It should definitely be a lesson for you. The just-enough worker appears busy so as not to take on any extra work.

Always request two computer monitors. One should face the door (your work monitor) and one should face a nonjudgmental wall that doesn't give a shit if you're online shopping or updating your resume. Always wear headphones and, if someone asks you for something, just pull them out, give them a panicked look, gesture to your computer, and be like, "I'd love to but do you think it can wait until next week?"

FORGET AMBITION

You're a small cog in the machine of life. The machine needs cogs. Shepherds breed and raise sheep for a living. When you drive through the English countryside and think, fuck these fields are so green and cute and I love all the stone walls crisscrossing everything let me stop and take a picture . . . Guess who's responsible for that view? Motherfucking shepherds. Literally the entire reason England is great, besides the queen's grandchildren and Jeremy Corbyn, is the men and women who herd sheep for a living. But there's no reality show called "Top Shepherd," is there? Know any shepherds? Of course not. Yet they make their country better, toiling away unseen since forever. That's you. A small cog in a giant machine of life. Doing just enough to keep the world turning. Comforting, isn't it?

EMAILS:
Answering 25 percent is enough

"You could say I was too lazy to calculate, so I invented the computer."
—KONRAD ZUSE

Thanks to whoever the asshole was that invented email. Al Gore, maybe? It's super convenient but also it never ends. You know the stories about mailmen who go off the rails because the mail never stops? That's all of us, now. Welcome to the crushing onslaught of your inbox. Hello, anxiety. The secret is to delete most of them. I had a boss that did this. His theory was that if it was important they'd email again. If not, he'd avoided having to deal with it. He also did this with utility bills and things like legal summons. So do whatever works for you. The point is that probably 50 percent of the shit in your inbox right now is just newsletters, marketing emails, and notifications about upcoming trips or events. Delete.

satisficieny
tip

Write your emails at night and then set them to
send at like 6 a.m. the following morning.
Everyone will think you're up early getting shit
done. By the time you wake up and start work
you'll already be ahead of the game.
There's also some kind of bullshit respect for
"morning people;" while I don't agree that anyone
should buy into that idea, it's a good way
to acknowledge the oppressive system we all labor
under while subverting it to your own advantage.

SALARY:
Quitting your job means more money

We're brought up to value loyalty. Work hard at the same job for years, keep your head down, prove yourself to the boss, and you'll be rewarded. Right? This attitude is actually losing you money. Instead of working harder at the same job, you need to work more efficiently by job-hopping your way to a raise. Studies found that staying at the same job for two years or more nets you 50 percent less money over your lifetime. Why is that? When you leave a job you can negotiate a better salary, and when you leave that job, you can negotiate an even better one. These kind of salary bumps vastly outpace the regular kind of raise you'd get if you stayed in the same job.

Take it from me. I've had about thirty minimum wage jobs over my (short, young, nubile) lifespan. I've been a barista at a ski resort, an inventory manager[*] at an amusement park, a waitress at establishments where the regulars would try and sell me gold chains, and one of those door-to-door canvassers that asks you for money. (Never give money to those people). I've worked the box office for an arts festival and cleaned dorm rooms for a university. If you think university students won't store a semester's worth of piss in two liter bottles for you to find in their closet, you'd be wrong. Each job paid a tiny bit better than the last, and now I'm a writer and I'm making so much money it's incredible. To everyone getting an arts degree right now—take heart. You, too, can earn slightly above the minimum wage.

....

* This sounds like a real job but basically it involved me—hungover—in a storage shed, making sure other employees didn't steal boxes of frozen bananas to sell to unsuspecting tourists so they could pocket the cash.

satisficieng tip

Get a new job and enjoy an instant raise.
But not one of those pyramid marketing schemes
selling essential oils and fat-blasting body wraps
and sex toys and storage boxes online.
Your friends don't want to buy that shit from you,
trust me.

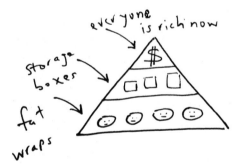

TAXES:
Filing them is enough so don't lose your shit over it

When I lived in rural South Carolina about fifteen years ago, there was a little bookstore in a nearby town that had a lot of Southern-pride-related items. You know the kind of items I mean. The store also had a lot of educational flyers and booklets and things about how the state was technically a country because it hadn't officially surrendered after the Civil War. Turns out the owner of this little bookstore (who referred to me as a Yankee) was also part of the local secessionist movement. He was basically the kind of stereotype Canadians might imagine when asked about the rural South. The point is that when I think of people who refuse to pay taxes and who hate "big government," I think of that guy.

Anyway, if you work and live somewhere you must pay taxes. This money goes into a collective pot and helps pay for new carpets in the White

House. It also pays the salaries of police, teachers, and fire departments across the nation. If you're in Canada, it pays the salaries of doctors and nurses, too. Every time a city worker fixes a sinkhole in Tallahassee, it's courtesy of American taxpayers. Every time a guy in Somerset drinks too much cider and punches a streetlight, it's replaced at taxpayer expense. See how that works?

But filing your taxes is also incredibly fucking complicated and stressful and people think way too much about this bullshit. No one should be scouring their credit card bill for things they can expense like the carpal-tunnel-prevention glove they bought online because their wrist hurt that one time and they lay awake that night stressed that their arms were about to age out before the rest of them.

So, unless you live anonymously on a sailboat in Key West (try collecting child support from me now, Linda!) or belong to one of those self-declared free nations and live in a cabin in the woods eating squirrels, you've got to do the bare minimum. Go online, do a free tax software thing the best you can, and click submit. If the government decides to come for you then whatever. Good luck I guess. There's probably another book that deals with what to do at that point.

satisficieny
tip

Download one of those apps that lets you take
pictures of your receipts and files them.
This is an earnest tip. I haven't actually done it yet,
but I've heard it's useful. Actually, my phone
storage is full. It's a problem. How are we
designing AI robots capable of starting a nuclear
war and Hyperloop prototypes to get us from
Calgary to Mexico City in under an hour, but
I can't keep 97,000 photos of my cat on my phone
without it maxing out my storage?

Quiz
what kind of overachiever are you?

1. What word best describes your morning routine?

  A. Sleep
  B. Coffee
  C. Jogging

chill pills

2. When it comes to food, you're like:

  A. Brunch then drinks then dinner
  B. Hamburgers or Hamburger Helper
  C. Apple

3. Has anyone ever told you to "take a chill pill?" (This may only apply to people alive in the '90s.)

  A. Never. I'm a very chill person.
  B. Once at my wedding and a few times when we renovated the kitchen.
  C. I have a prescription for chill pills. It doesn't help.

4. When it comes to answering emails:

   A. My auto reply is always on: "I'm on vacation but will get back to you as soon as I can."

   B. I try and reply within 24 hours of receipt.

   C. I have three unread emails in my inbox right now and it's frankly driving me nuts.

Answer Key:

Mostly As: Sloth. Like the sloth, you're excellent at doing just enough. You don't expend a lot of energy over bullshit. It takes you a week to get to the bathroom. I'm surprised you even have the energy to read this book! Now go take a nap.

Mostly Bs: Rhinoceros. No one really knows exactly what your deal is. Are you chill or are you sort of violent? What do you think about at night? A promotion? Forget it. Just be yourself! Which is, what? You like mud and rivers and stuff, probably.

Mostly Cs: Mosquito. You're trying too hard, moving too fast, irritating the shit out of everyone around you, and for what? What's the rush? You know we're all still going to die, right? No matter how fast you try and escape death, it's coming for all of us.

3.

Just Enough in Relationships

"I am a very lazy man, so, for me, the dream is to be at home on the chair with my family."
—ANDREA BOCELLI

There are a shit-ton of books out there about improving your relationships and your love life. There are articles about the best places for a romantic couple's vacation and the best kind of sensual massage and guidelines for how often you should have date night or the kind of lingerie that drives him wild or tips for how to listen.

It's all about how we should be doing more. Not satisfied? Try harder. It's the same cycle we fall into when worrying about why we aren't happy with our jobs, our house, our fingernails (we all bite them). Stop worrying about trying harder and admit you're already doing just enough.

Anyway, a good thing to keep in mind is that most relationships fail, and I'm pretty sure it's not because you didn't book that trip to Cabo. Or maybe because you did book it and it was a disaster. The point is, if trying hard works half the time, why not do less with the same outcome?

LOVE:
It's about trendy British television

The joy of doing just enough in love isn't about planning an expensive vacation where you'd end up obsessing over the best Instagram post: both your hands making a heart in front of a Mexico sunset? Your feet in a cabana that overlooks the ocean? Two frozen cocktails with orchids in them next to a pair of sunglasses and your straw hat that says "Find Me at the Beach"?

No. In the just-enough world we drink white wine and watch British TV shows. Honestly I want the BBC to make every program forever. Everyone drinks tea and talks about the bloke

down at the local who turned out to be a serial
killer, and there's always shots of the beautiful
but sinister countryside to make you feel safe
and cozy on your couch. I'm not saying don't go
on vacation. I'm just saying finding joy in your
current relationship is easier than that. (Unless
it's a shitty relationship, in which case, try and
have a baby quickly. They fix everything).

WHEN JUST ENOUGH IS TOO MUCH

....

My friend was in a terrible relationship with a guy who was into alternative facts. It took a lot of mental energy to believe that he was actually in the CIA or that the porn DVD (this was awhile ago, obvi) actually belonged to his brother. But she tried. Once he pretended to move to another country and would call her from a new phone number to tell her all about his exciting new job. Turns out he was actually living in his parents' basement.

This is depressing because it's obviously insane and what the fuck. But anyone who's been in a terrible relationship probably has put up with (hopefully less weird) shit. Ideally, you learned from it and found someone better.

If you're still in a shitty relationship, my condolences. Try not to get married. Let it flame out in spectacular fashion like my friend's did when she came home from vacation and he'd changed the locks and let his new girlfriend move in.

DATING:
Shave the beard

According to the Bureau of Labor Statistics, 50.2 percent of American adults are single. Which means about half of the nation's adults are looking for love (a conclusion you'll draw if you're as good at analyzing statistics as I am). But dating is fucking stressful, especially when there's a lot of pressure to enter into a partnership in the first place. That's why a lot of people just opt out of the romance race altogether and adopt things like monkeys to keep them company (looking at you, Emily Carr and Justin Bieber). I get it. We're expected to dedicate time to finding true love, and we've already got a lot of other shit to do, like washing our pears.*

The just-enough dating model is all about going on enough dates to keep friends and family off your back. But importantly, it's not so much dating that your full-time job becomes interviewing for your next fuck. The best way to

* see page 45

maximize your dates and minimize the amount of time you spend thinking about dating is to give a drunk married friend your phone and let them swipe right for a while. You're doing them a favor, and it saves you the hassle of doing it yourself. And fellas, if you really want to meet someone online, shave your beard. Beardless men are 37 percent more likely to find a match.

Go on vacation. One-night stands are super easy to have when you're in another country. And you can dine out on the story of how you met—at a nightclub in Amsterdam and fooled around until about 5 a.m. when you both went to get breakfast tacos—for a long time.

EMOTIONALLY:

Not being a dick

Love Hacks
not Shacks

If you want satisficiency in your relationship, try to not be an asshole. I'm not a doctor or any kind of professional, but this super-smart psychologist came up with a series of "love hacks" (tried and tested in his "relationship laboratory") that can improve your love life with just a few simple techniques. For those people who are overwhelmed at the thought of reconnecting in a meaningful way with their partner: take heart. There's a hack for that. "Touch your partner" is one of the key bits of advice. "Celebrate small victories" is another. Also "don't jump to negative conclusions." What does this mean for you and your FIB score? Basically, if he whittles an unrealistic image of you in your backyard elm tree, let it slide. If she offers to pluck a silky wayward hair from your perineum, then thank her for her service. If one of you is arrested for running a Ponzi scheme like it's 2008, then try and forgive and forget. Easy! If you hate each other, however, then being nice to one another might be hard. But then you've got other shit to worry about.

PHYSICALLY:
Low-level fondling

As you get older and your arm skin starts to sag and you find your partner's views on the best way to cook scrambled eggs to be extremely irritating, it can be hard to feel sexy and find the time for physical intimacy.

Hand jobs are an easy way to keep shit sexy without having to take off all your clothes or put in a lot of effort. Hand jobs are also great if you're a teenager and need to keep shit on the DL in your car or living room. You can even do it over his pants on the subway or something. Points for being naughty, and you both have something interesting to think about on the hour-long ride from Brooklyn to Queens or wherever you're headed. Also someone is definitely filming you so in a way you're spreading the love, which makes this a true win-win as long as you manage not to get arrested for public indecency (which, alas, may be a real problem on the subway. Also, people can get uptight on airplanes. You've been warned).

SOCIALLY:
Radiolab can wait

Interacting with the same person forever at all hours of the day can get exhausting. It's easy to search for an escape by watching videos of an owl being rescued from a wire fence or a turtle swimming away after being freed from a fishing net. These tiny moments of animal joy can save us from the monotony of life with someone whose fart scent you're overly familiar with. This is why earphones were invented. However, looking up from your phone screen gives the impression that you're listening. Same with taking out your earbuds when someone is talking to you. Your shitty political podcast can wait a few seconds while you agree that the new mirror really does make the room feel bigger. It's the little things that count here.

WEDDINGS:
No one gives a fuck about anything except the free booze

booze

If your relationship goes well then you'll likely get married at some point. So take science into account when you plan it: The cheaper the wedding, the more successful the marriage. Don't get carried away. According to economists at Emory University, couples who get married for less than $1,000 have the best odds for staying together. If your wedding costs more than $20,000, you're probably fucked. Or you're currently being fucked by your hot neighbor with a beard and a plaid shirt. Good for you. Anyway. You may feel that a wedding these days requires trendy wedding colors, his-and-hers donut sculptures, flower walls, a photo booth, and free bowling. It doesn't. What you need is an open bar. That's literally the only reason your guests are excited to attend your wedding. You can get married in an empty field with your guests sitting on hay bales in the hot sun while ticks latch on to their ankles. They don't care. Turn them loose on the open bar after your vows are done and watch the magic happen. If it's anything like my friend's wedding, you'll hopefully have to call an ambulance for one of your guests. He won't remember dropping his pint glass in the bathroom and passing out against the door and everyone having to gather around while the event staff unscrew the door from its hinges—but everyone else will. And they will remember it as a great wedding.

satisficieny tip

A while back a bunch of all-inclusive resorts
in Mexico got busted for putting moonshine in
brand-name booze bottles. It was cheaper for
them and the guests didn't notice. I'm not saying to
do that to save money at your wedding while still
impressing your guests with the Black Label Johnnie
Walker. But I'm not saying to not do it.

5.

Just Social Enough

"I can relax with bums because I am a bum. I don't like laws, morals, religions, rules. I don't like to be shaped by society."
—CHARLES BUKOWSKI

Life comes with annoying obligations, like feeding your kids, or paying your rent, or trying not to do heroin. Not everyone succeeds. But throw in the need to be friendly, to stay up to speed on your friend's mother's hip replacement, to know how to mix a fancy cocktail, to post something sappy about "Sibling Day" (yes, that's real), and even the above-average person gets overwhelmed. The just-enough method is here to help.

PARTIES:
Showing up is enough

People seem to hit this random age where going to parties is a kind of work. Remember in high school when you got invited to parties and you'd get super excited and secretly pour a bunch of your parents' peach schnapps into a water bottle and mix it with orange juice and sail out of the house in your best-yet-most casual high school outfit? Where I grew up we called them bush parties, because they'd be out in a field or forest somewhere and they usually involved some huge bonfire and lots of people from other high schools and maybe a DJ. You'd keep your fingers crossed you'd be able to share a cigarette with your crush and then spend the evening talking about how a friend of a friend got fingered behind the bushes. Anyway.

When you're eighteen, parties are not work. They are fucking fun. The world is open and you're free and everything is possible. When you hit your thirties, however, parties become a lot lamer (this is relative depending on your personality I guess. If you love talking about basement renovations, IVF, and anxiously waiting for the host to refill your wine glass, that's cool). Your parties become dinner parties and you're expected to bring a quinoa salad and wine and be able to talk about current events. It's exhausting.

Everyone knows that last-minute scramble that happens fifteen minutes after you were supposed to have left for the party. Fuck, it's a fortieth birthday and I didn't get them a card! Fuck, it's a first birthday party and we forgot to get them a thoughtful, educational board book! Fuck, we forgot to buy nice wine!

The secret to partying as you age: Just show the fuck up. That's the secret. You don't have to bring anything. Forget all those Pinterest boards that advertise the best kind of hostess gifts and the perfect type of ribbon for your homemade jam. You bring that kind of shit once, you become the person who brings homemade gifts

and you're fucked. That's a lot of pressure. Just be the person who shows up. It's the bare minimum, but it's the most important thing. And just imagine how much more enjoyable your evening will be if you don't spend the preceding hours worrying about what to bring and what you look like. Also, speaking of the bare minimum: If you have time before the party, google the Daily Mail and read all the headlines. That will provide you with lots of good dinner conversation. "This butt model with two million followers discovered a new type of jellyfish." "Did you hear about the Russian playboy who got his pet tiger a passport?" No one wants to rehash the current political situation or worry about the impending

nuclear holocaust. So don't worry if you can't remember who the current Secretary of Defense is. It's fine to talk about sharks instead.

If you're lucky enough to have the kind of life where parties are still fun and not an obligation—congrats. You probably live in Europe.

• satisficieny •
tip

Show up. Remember a fun fact or joke to tell everyone. Here's one: I had a dream I was a car muffler last night! Then when everyone is like, what the fuck, we don't care about your dreams it's literally the most boring thing you could talk about, you can be like, I woke up exhausted! This joke works better when everyone is drunk.

BOOZING:
Just enough is more than you think

One of the things about drinking, social drug use, having children, exercising, etc., is that people have always got shit to say about it. Hot yoga five times a week? Fucking irritating. Three kids? You've already got two. Another beer? You get the idea. Everyone's always worried about how much is too much. The point is you should do whatever you feel like. The joy is in doing just enough of whatever it is you want.

I'm not talking about people that have health or addiction issues obviously. Hard science and Western medicine are here to help you, despite what your aunt posts about lemon oil curing cancer. I'm talking about people who just do what makes them feel good in the moment because it's fun and they're having a good time. Plus, I'm here to tell you that smart people drink more. *Psychology Today* notes that even taking into account a ton of demographic variables like sex, religion, education, and class, intelligent children in the US and UK grow up to consume more booze than their less bright counterparts. Sound like you? Thought so.

But the world is full of tests and quizzes and advice about how much is too much to drink at a party. Isn't it wonderful to have so many rules and guidelines? Something else to worry about! I'm not drinking so are people noticing that? I'm drinking a lot so are people noticing that? So here's a handy system to know whether or not you're drinking too much at a party.

Quiz

how much drinking is too much?

Are you having fun?

  A. yes

  B. no

Answer key:

A. If you are having fun, keep doing whatever you're doing.

B. If you're not having fun, stop drinking, drink more, or leave the party. You're an adult. Do whatever the fuck you want. Aren't these quizzes irritating as shit? Unless you're a tweenager and you're trying to determine if your crush likes you, these kind of "are you normal" quizzes are mostly designed to make you feel like shit, just like your doctor when they ask you how many units of alcohol you drink per week, and you have to lie because honestly who can figure out how many units are in three bottles of wine?

BONUS:

Cocktails that don't require a mixology degree from Hipster U

All good social events start with a good, easy-to-make cocktail. Or at least, many mediocre social events are made bearable by booze. Forget the artisanal blueberry shrub, organic ice, and smoked juniper garnish, and forget just handing someone a can of beer. Just-enough hosts, take note: Here are some easy, half-assed recipes* for making strong drinks that require three ingredients or less. Drink these and have a slightly better time on your date!

....

* For more of these, check out my book *Cocktails for Drinkers*. Part of doing just enough is working the cross promotion.

Schnapps To-Go

This is a drink for anyone who's tired of
pretentious cocktails made with frothed egg
whites from free-range chickens and bark
from Finnish birch trees. It's sweet, fruity,
and easy.

Makes however many of these you feel like drinking

Peach Schnapps
Orange juice

Mix these up in whatever proportion
you like in a water bottle. Add ice if you
want it cold. You can take this drink anyplace,
even a bush party.

Paloma

Straight tequila is great for those evenings you
don't want to remember. But some
of us like a sophisticated tequila cocktail.
One made with soda pop. Drink up,
fancy pants. You're basically Kate Middleton.

Makes one large drink or two small drinks

6 ounces Fresca (or any grapefruit-flavored soda)

2 ounces tequila

Add the ingredients into a glass. Stir it up. Add
a lime wedge and some ice cubes and serve.
Repeat until you start talking about religion at
the dinner party.

Vodka Soda

You don't have to be an aspiring actress living
in Los Feliz to enjoy these basically
calorie-free cocktails. You can also be working
in finance. Either way, this is a strong, straight-
forward drink that looks good on you, bro.

Makes 1 large drink or 2 small ones

4 ounces vodka

8 ounces soda

Add the ingredients into a glass and stir. Toss in
an ice cube and a wedge of lemon. Congratulate
yourself on your recent callback/bonus.

White Wine

Wine is made from grapes and comes in a bottle or a box. There's just the one ingredient, so it's a great recipe to practice with.

Makes one large drink

1 bottle of wine

Open the wine and let it breathe. Just kidding. Pour it in a large glass immediately and drink it up like a suburban housewife.

SOCIAL MEDIA:
Forget filters and like everything

Social media channels require a lot of upkeep, we're told. We're expected to use "social" to engage our audience with consistent, curated content, signature filters, strategic tagging, oh my God, whatever, I can never finish those articles that tell you how to be better at social media. There's always Nine Key Things and one of them is about how you should post at the same time every day and yet posting a photo of my cat or my sandwich at 1 p.m. every weekday is a dumb fucking idea. Who are those people who are "successful" on social media anyway? We know that many of these accounts pay for followers ($10 for 1,000 followers is the going rate) and also work full time convincing those fake followers how great their lives are in order to attract advertisers so they can sustain this clusterfuck until they are too old to photograph well in a bikini or board shorts.

The point is that unless you're a public figure or social media is a form of income for you (doubtful), there are no rules about how much to post and what to post. Liberating, right? There's no way to be successful at it. It's just basically a bulletin board for your life that maybe a hundred people care about. And it's kind of a necessity in this day and age. How else will you know which of your high school friends turned out to be racist?

So stop worrying about editing your photos or crafting funny status updates. Here's what real people actually post about and it's why social media is the greatest:

- The backyard hibiscus.

- "My little helper." This is a kid with a spatula or something.

- The cat is ready for winter.

- My kid is growing up so fast. Laugh/cry emoji!

- Mom's birthday.

- Sibling day. How the fuck did that become a thing?

- Their car/motorcycle.

- A meme designed by the Russians to sow discord in America. It's usually your great aunt that posts these.

Nobody wants curated shit! They want your real life. The divorce. The post baby-belly. The pie you made. Your thoughts on why minimum wage is fine where it is. With that said, if you can't be bothered to post, be sure to like.

satisficieny tip

Like everything. Photo of a baby? Like.
Photo of someone's new deck? Like.
Inside joke you don't get? Like. This strategy
requires basically no work or forethought
and it makes you seem engaged in other people's
lives and they will appreciate it. Success!

do not Instagram

_5._

Just Enough Arts and Culture

"You speak an infinite deal of nothing."
—WILLIAM SHAKESPEARE

There's too much content to consume. I'm sick of the expectation that to be a useful member of society we have to keep up with all the latest things. New shows about the royal family, New York in the '70s, and old reruns that you just need to watch again (looking at you, *Party of Five*) are begging for our attention. There are new books, movies, apps, and brands that you don't have time to learn about. Forget about consuming content. Focus on quick headlines and fast facts that make it seem like you've got (1) holiday cheer, (2) more than a passing knowledge of the new tax bill, and (3) a smashing trip to Lisbon planned. No one will be the wiser.

CREATIVE ENDEAVORS:
Writing four pages is enough

I'm saying this to save you some time: Your screenplay isn't very good, so don't work too hard on it. Everyone in the film industry probably knows this already, because 95 percent of their job is listening to their accountant and teacher friends go on about how they're writing a screenplay which is definitely bad. "It's a heist film set in a dystopian future starring a disgruntled housewife and her nursing home friend—a kind of *Fried Green Tomatoes* meets *Waterworld*." I tried writing a screenplay once. I thought: I've seen a movie. I can write things down. Whatever. Then you get four pages in and go: Fuck. A lot of things have to happen in a screenplay. It isn't like a novel, where you can win a National Book Award for your beautiful evocation of post-divorce life in a Tennessee cabin with your dog where there are literally ten pages of description about what the Smoky Mountains looked like through your haze of whiskey nostalgia tears.

No. In a screenplay people have to say things and do things and there must be conflict and resolution and it can't be cliché or have stilted dialogue ("Mary, why are you holding that knife? I already cut the cake. *Mary!*") and there can't be plot holes either. Not that I'd know. I got four pages in and was like, fuck this. Leave it to the professionals. And so should you. Same goes for novels.

What you are very good at is watching TV and films and reading books. You're a successful consumer. And good for you! Your viewership keeps thousands of people in the industry employed.

● satisficieny ●
tip

Write a few pages and get it out of your system. Then binge-watch a few actual good shows. The industry needs your support and appreciates it. They don't appreciate your screenplay. Assholes, right?

BOOKS:
Read just enough weird shit to be interesting at a social event

"Always read something that will make you look good if you die in the middle of it."
—P.J. O'ROURKE

When you live in New York, you meet a lot of people with degrees in literature who read things you've never heard of. Novels reimagining Chopin's wife as a modern-day ballet dancer in Yonkers. Talking to these kinds of people about these kinds of books is difficult because you don't know what the fuck they're talking about. "Have you read Zadie Smith's latest essay for the *Lon-*

don Review of Books? It's all about MDMA, The Smiths, and life on a housing estate in Hackney in the 1980s." You just finished the novel about a Parisian hat-maker that likely took place during WW II. Oprah loved it. It has 4,000 five-star reviews online. You thought it was the current trendy book to be reading and it was fine. You liked it. But there are 400 current trendy books right now. This is one of them (well done).

Reading all the latest "it" books has become another source of stress. The just-enough philosophy for reading is as follows: Find a niche and make that your thing. You love dragons? Run with it. You like BDSM? Trust me, people will want to know more about the last book you read on the subject. Super into Brazilian flash fiction? Run with it.

The most interesting people at parties are the ones who know weird shit about weird, unhip topics. Oh, you want to know about animals that practice symbiosis? You'd like to discuss Germany's obsession with Westerns? Have you heard about this history of Newfoundland and Labrador and how it almost became part of the US? Let me tell you all about formaldehyde and mole skulls. Etc. The next time you're at a party and someone asks you if you've read X's latest, tell them about the surfing-themed poetry book you bought from a guy in a yurt in Joshua Tree National Park. It was printed in all caps and hand stapled and cost you twenty bucks. But it was interesting and now you have a fun story and you will seem well read because you read so much that you have time to read the weird shit no one knows about.

satisficieny tip

If you must, read the summary of the hottest
new books online. Then when someone mentions
about how it won an award you can say, ahh,
is that the one about the three generations of circus
bears in Ukraine? And you'll appear to know
what the fuck you're talking about without having
read a nonsense book just because NPR loved it.

mouse

TRAVELING:
The Amalfi Coast is fine but so is the local coffee shop

"A good traveler has no fixed plans and is not intent on arriving."

—LAO TZU

"Travel influencers" and sorority girls who also love Marilyn Monroe post quotes from Lao Tzu while traveling the world on someone else's dime. The world's tourist sites are full of these kinds of performative travelers, always dressed in clean, flowing clothes and straw hats. Their timelines are packed with beautiful, sanitized travels pics that always seem to happen at sunset with nary a missed train or overpriced bottle of water or sunstroke to be seen. They showcase the kind of images that make the rest of us feel like jumping out the window of a Midtown high-rise or over the counter of our minimum wage job and giving a speech about capitalism or reparations or the 1 percent. "Postcard from San Sebastian," they'll write. "Besos!"

Most people don't do European cruises to Montenegro or hike to Petra in Jordan or drink coffee in Venice or bicycle in Chile unless it's for a honeymoon or special occasion. Traveling is expensive and tiring and it requires a lot of planning. So forget your spreadsheets and wallet full of foreign currency and the printout of the train schedules and the sunscreen and malaria shots. It's too much, and you'll never keep up with blonde Lilly from Australia and her fourteen bikinis and 20 million followers. Anyway, I heard she was arrested for posing nude at some sacred temple.

Doing just enough travel is key. If it suits you, I recommend seasonal work. That's where you travel somewhere like a ski resort or a golf and country club that will hire you for around six months in exchange for room and board and a paycheck. You will meet cool people from all over who will comfort you when you get arrested for underage drinking or who you'll drive to the abortion clinic or any number of intimate things that will bond you all together forever. And isn't that a lot more authentic than spending a week in Croatia and taking 400 selfies? Barring that, take a train somewhere. Trains are fun old-timey travel and are pretty cheap. Or visit a weird local museum, like the one about your town's violin cemetery. It's actually quite sad. So many violins, most of them young, most buried without proper ceremony—anonymous. Until now!

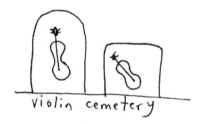

violin cemetery

satisficieny tip

Next time you're waiting in line for your morning coffee, close your eyes and pretend you're in France. Cheap, easy, hard to Instagram.
The best and most authentic type of travel, no?

HOLIDAYS:
You've got other shit to do

Holidays come with a lot of expectations. Everything must be themed appropriately, from your turkey napkins to your Chanukkah lawn ornaments. You must entertain or be entertained. You must dress appropriately.

You must avoid this. By doing just enough for the holidays, you'll impart a festive feeling without creating massive expectations for the following year. Remember, people learn to expect what you deliver. Go overboard one year and you'll look lazy the next.

New Year's Eve: This is the most overrated holiday. My uncle, a recovering alcoholic, calls it amateur night. Get a bottle of champagne and stay in. Do not attempt to throw a party.

Valentine's Day: Get them a card and write something sexy or heartfelt. The card is the most important thing and literally the easiest. If you do get your loved one a present, don't fucking post about it on social media. It negates the niceness of the present. So you sprung for roses and a hotel with a hot tub. Whatever. No one needs to see your girlfriend lounging in it naked and covered in bubbles.

April Fool's Day: Don't celebrate this unless you're under twelve. If I get one more jokey email on April 1st from some company launching a new line of eyewear for dogs or a new ride service for babies, I swear to God . . . No one likes this holiday except sociopaths.

Cinco de Mayo: Raise a glass of good tequila to celebrate the Mexican army's defeat of the French in the Battle of Puebla. Know that if you're wearing a sombrero, it's too much.

Canada Day: Grab a 24, some ketchup chips, a red shirt, and watch the fireworks. No one cares about your homemade Nanaimo bars, your pin-the-mustache on Jagmeet Singh game, and your canoe handcarved by the Hudson's Bay Company. All Canadians need on July 1st is beer and maybe a lake.

Ketchup chips

American Independence Day: Same as above but with a case of beer, some hamburgers, and a flag T-shirt. All anyone expects here is a barbecue. You could have a barbecue in an empty field with nary an American flag to be seen, and it would be just enough.

Rosh Hashanah: Sound the shofar, eat some apples dipped in honey. Forget the New Year's cards—they set a precedent, and the year you decide to stop sending them everyone will be offended.

Yom Kippur: Take the day off work. There's no way to overdo this. Just enjoy it (respectfully).

Halloween: I'm probably in the minority on this one because people fucking love Halloween. But your inflatable lawn ghost isn't necessary. Get a pumpkin and carve it. Put a candle in it and set it outside. Instant Halloween. Everyone knows you're giving out candy but also that you've got other shit to do than hang spiderwebs over your entire property. Also, dress as a cat.

one jack-o-lantern will suffice

Canadian Thanksgiving: Order in.

American Thanksgiving: Order in. You make a turkey one year and you're fucked. Everyone will expect a feast every following year for forever and eventually you'll snap and suggest spending Thanksgiving in Reno so you don't have to cook.

Chanukkah: Matzo dough is tricky. Crackers are enough.

Christmas: I knew someone who decorated four Christmas trees every year—three at the main house and one at their vacation property. Not to be Grinch-y, but that's too many fucking trees. Have one tree. Hang a stocking. Play some Christmas carols. It's all you need to evoke the spirit of Christmas and it's easy to clean up later.

A note on holiday dress codes: Buy a black outfit and wear it to everything. Halloween? You're a cat. Funeral? You're in mourning. Christmas? You're wearing elf earrings!

6.

Just Enough Health and Beauty

"If I'm going to be a mess—might as well be a hot mess."

—MINDY KALING

We all feel pressure to look good. Sometimes I pass a beautiful woman on the street and I wonder how the hell they look so put together. No wrinkles or lint or scuffed shoes or T-zone shine. Just perfection. Money and a lot of spare time are probably the key here. But looking good is a slippery and expensive slope. You start dying your hair and in order to maintain it you've got to dye it every month or so forever. You can't afford that.

Just shower a few times a week and brush your hair before leaving the house. Don't get anyone's expectations too high. That way when you put on a nice sweater and some lip balm for your coworker's bridal shower, everyone will give you compliments. Anyway, you look fantastic as is.

WORKING OUT:

If you work out, put this book down right now and walk away

"For fast-acting relief, try slowing down."
—LILY TOMLIN

Once in high school, I was eating a cold cut trio sub for lunch. This overachieving spark from the track and field team (and a bunch of other team sports) told me I was brave for eating it. "That's so brave," she said. I had no idea what the fuck she was talking about. Turns out the sub has a lot of calories. Or the meat is made from animal assholes and couch cushions or something. Anyway, that person now lives in a healthy city where everyone bikes everywhere and she's a reiki practitioner probably and we are not friends on social media. The point is that there are different kinds of people in the world. She is a what society calls an overachiever (newsflash: choosing to not eat cold cuts is fine but talking about not eating cold cuts makes you literally the most

just enough

boring person alive). I am someone who does just enough. Taking a walk is enough. Remembering to stretch or turn off the laptop after 47 hours is enough. Remembering to call it quits after two bottles of wine is enough. Are you alive? That's perfect. Maybe you're also sick of people telling you about ten quick and easy ways to cut belly fat or how to make a whole lunch out of lettuce and acai berries or how to train for a half marathon. Which is why the "working out" section of this book is so short. Go for a walk, if you want. I don't give a shit.

satisficieny tip

Laughing is actually healthier than jogging,
according to one German doctor. Laughing
produces serotonin which makes you feel happy and
relaxed. So next time someone asks if you
work out, think about the latest comedy special
you watched online and say yes.

relaxing
blob

SLEEP:
How to get just enough

"I love sleep. My life has the tendency to fall apart when I'm awake, you know?"
—ERNEST HEMINGWAY

I happen to be an excellent sleeper. Once, in university, I lived in a house with five other girls (don't ever do this) and one of the girls thought I had a sleeping disorder because I slept until noon. No consideration of the fact that I'd been out the night before until 3 a.m. Turns out, if you go to bed at 8 p.m., you wake up fairly early, nerd. The point is we all have different sleep habits. Sloths sleep anywhere from 10 to 18 hours a day, for example. Yet getting just enough sleep—the kind where you wake up naturally, refreshed, and ready to roll—has a bit of a stigma. In our world obsessed with success, if you're sleeping more than seven or eight hours a night, you mustn't have a lot to do, right? Getting just enough sleep is something to be embarrassed about. It means you're lazy.

Not getting enough sleep, however, is admirable. What a fantastic example of a busy and accomplished human being you are! I'm so busy, I can get by on just six hours, these people say modestly, with a shrug. I don't have time for the human weakness that is sleeping. Yet getting less than seven hours of sleep is considered sleep deprivation (a form of actual torture) and can have serious effects on your health (new parents know this). In fact, adults 45 years or older who get less than six hours of sleep a night are 200 percent more likely than their sleepier peers to have a heart attack or stroke. So, congrats on getting up early to answer emails. The person who slept until noon is going to outlive you.

So quit overdoing it. Quit this obsession with being conscious all the time—your body will thank you. Getting a good night's sleep can help improve your happiness levels, your concentration, improve your short-term memory, and even help you build muscle. Also dreaming is fun and is linked to creativity. Do you remember your dreams? Once I dreamed I rescued Tony Blair from a plane crash.

So, in the words of a popular children's book: Go the fuck to sleep.

satisficieny tip

Drink a lot and pass out on the floor.
Or take a sleeping pill. Wake up when you goddamn feel like it.

sleeping pills

BEAUTY ROUTINE:
8 items or fewer

"The only way I'd be caught without makeup is if my radio fell in the bathtub while I was taking a bath and electrocuted me and I was in between makeup at home. I hope my husband would slap a little lipstick on me before he took me to the morgue."
—DOLLY PARTON

The average woman uses sixteen beauty products before leaving the house in the morning and spends around $300,000 on beauty products in her lifetime.

On a recent flight, sitting in coach, I sat next to what was certainly an above-average lady. We got to talking about her skincare routine. She suggested I get a monthly facial.

She also suggested that I start using La Mer products. For those who don't know, La Mer is a luxury skincare brand that costs $8 billion

an ounce and is made of finely ground mermaid nipples. Then she told me about how they'd recently sold their Hawaii house so they only had three houses now: New York, New Jersey, and Florida. She was the kind of person you know exists because you have television and Instagram but who you'd never meet in real life because you live in a basement apartment and don't get invited to charity galas for increased awareness of how Lyme disease affects labradoodles. She looked great. And she was only medium rich. I mean, she was still flying commercial, even if she did have an aisle seat. If you went up another level of wealth (the 1 percent of the 1 percent, say) you'd likely find someone who gets daily anti-aging blood transfusions and who recommends investing in a replacement set of DNA, preferably plant-based. Mushroom mitochondria are the best, darling!

So for the rest of us, we need a beauty routine to help us look awake and showered, but not one so over the top that we look like selfies are our full-time job. The just-enough beauty routine should take no more than five minutes: wash off last night's makeup you were too drunk to remove at 3 a.m., slap on some moisturizer, and fill in your eyebrows, I guess. I'm not some YouTube beauty tutorial expert, but I do know bushy brows are "in" right now. And drink a glass of water.

No matter your beauty routine, take comfort in the fact that today is the best you will ever look—it's all downhill from here. Until the Silicon Valley libertarians decide to completely flout whatever government regulations exist currently keeping us from an AI takeover, and invent a way to implant your brain cells into a customized robot so we can live forever, everyone is going to get old(er) looking and die. In 100 years, you and everyone you know will be dead. A great reason to have another glass of wine or not go to yoga today.

• satisficieny •
tip

I recommend wearing sunscreen. So does science.
Sunscreen is cheap so you have no excuse.
It's like, science for the masses! It's too late for me,
though, because I really loved tanning beds
when I was younger.

is your beauty routine "rich lady bonkers"
or just enough?

1. What best describes your skincare routine?

A. Ten-step Korean skincare all the way. Rice oil face wash, exfoliator, toner, serum, moisturizer, eye cream, primer, sunscreen. And I only fuck with sexy ingredients like snail extract. (Also Botox, bitches!)

B. Sunscreen, when I remember. Also some lady at the makeup counter recommended a highlighter for my cheekbones. Whatever.

C. Soap. I'm not an asshole.

2. When you grocery shop you look for:

A. Actually, my personal chef does the shopping, keeping in mind my list of no-nos which include sugar, gluten, soy, dairy, and enjoyment.

B. Those little hybrid tangerine nectarines in little bags and some kale, I guess.

C. Soda pop and breath mints. And anything microwavable.

3. Multivitamins are important to you because:

A. I own a multivitamin company. Have you heard about the benefits of turmeric tablets?

B. Sometimes vitamin D is a nice pick me up in the middle of winter.

C. Vitamins are a scam, right? There's no oversight in that industry. You could literally be eating chalk.

4. Lipstick is:

A. Organic, nutrient-rich with added jojoba oils, and comes in thirty shades.

B. Fine. I have a red lipstick I bust out when I'm drunk.

C. Pointless. Lip balm for life.

5. Your retirement plan is basically:

A. Ten-hour sessions of floating salt water therapy in my private estate in the south of France, followed by elderflower water enemas.

B. Arizona maybe? I heard it's cheap out there and I can maintain my tan. Hopefully the overloaded electricity grid hasn't collapsed due to climate change by the time I get there.

C. Government-run nursing home, if I live that long.

Answer Key:

Mostly As: Congratulations. You're Gwyneth Paltrow.

Mostly Bs: You're doing just enough beauty maintenance. Your half-assed approach to looking your best gives you more time for the important shit in life, like putting things in your online shopping basket and not buying them. It's the thrill of anticipation, right?

Mostly Cs: Congrats on opting out of all of society's bullshit. You still look great but you probably don't give a fuck either way. Weird you even did this quiz, though.

DIET:

Part-time paleo, mostly vegan, generally gluten-free

Life is too hard and short and difficult to stick to diets and follow eating fads. Doing anything 100 percent forever is setting yourself up for failure. Eighty percent adherence is enough. Have you ever met someone who has been a vegetarian their whole life? Someone who hasn't eaten bread in fifteen years? Someone who eats paleo for every single meal? Not likely. Usually they tried some fad diet for a few years in university (vegetarians). Or when they moved to LA (no bread). Or for those two years they were into CrossFit (paleo). But try going to a nursing home and finding someone there who's still vegan. I asked my grandmother once if she ever considered being vegetarian and she said something like, "We ate what we ate and if we didn't boy, we'd be in trouble." That's probably because she grew up in the Midwest with not very much money and her parents would have freaked out if she'd suddenly decided potato salad and corn had too many carbs or that cows had souls. In fact, 97 percent of dieters regain the weight they lost within three years because dieting is pointless. Anyway, it's very exhausting to stick to something like only eating leaves forever. Diets should be a guideline*—aim for 80 percent adherence. Being a vegetarian and also eating hotdogs is fine.

satisficieny
tip

Be a cool vegan who loves scrambled eggs
and puts whole milk in their coffee.
Be a paleo guy that also loves pizza. You'll feel
better, and your friends will like you more.

....

* Unless you have legitimate health issues. A friend's dad once had a heart attack and the ER doctor told him he had to eat more healthy foods. Then he asked his kids to bring him Wendy's while he was in hospital awaiting his triple bypass. This was the same guy who kept sundae glasses chilled in his freezer. Every night he'd get a glass out, fill it with ice cream and top it with chocolate syrup. No idea if he's alive still.

DEATH: Drown in a vat of cookie dough, if possible

"If life must not be taken too seriously, then so neither must death"
—SAMUEL BUTLER

Because we must be successful in all aspects of our lives, there is now a shit-ton of pressure on us to die properly in our old age. We must now prepare to have a "good death." Like the thought of dying of old age or illness isn't stressful enough. Oh, your loved one suffered? Too bad. Be better prepared next time.

Dying in a responsible way used to mean simple shit like going out with an updated legal will, a do-not resuscitate form on file, your organ donor card signed, and your debts paid. Now, however, we must prepare to die correctly. So brush up on planning a responsible death with articles like "Scientifically, What's the Best Way to Die?" (guillotine) and "Seven Keys to a

Good Death" (experience as little pain as possible). Once you've read the literature, you'll be encouraged to pick out your preferred retirement home, nursing home, and hospice. Definitely plan to declutter your home and give away all your belongings to ensure your descendants aren't burdened with all your bullshit. (No one wants your china, your VHS tapes, your thirty old mobile phones.) Hand-stitched doilies? Fuck them.

Sounds stressful? It is. Why shouldn't you leave all that shit for everyone left behind to deal with? Why should you be forced to give away everything you worked your entire life to acquire? Good question. The just-enough method of preparing for death involves lots of Post-it notes. Write the name of whomever you'd like to have your grandfather clock (if you're 98 and live in a haunted house) when you're gone and affix it to the clock. Easy. Then when your kids come over and see that Gary is getting the clock rather than

Harriet you can work the just-enough method
of parenting: let the kids fight it out.

satisficieny
tip

Aim to go out in a blaze of glory under a
pile of newspapers that toppled over on you in a
house filled with everything you own.
Then at least you get an article about yourself in the
paper after you're gone. Or invest in a guillotine.

THE GENTLE ART SWEDISH DEATH CLEANING, OR *DÖSTÄDNING*

....

Swedish death cleaning is a lame new fad with an admittedly cool name. In a new twist on *The Life-Changing Magic of Tidying Up*, *döstädning* suggests a method that is actually *death-changing*. (But not really, because once you're dead *it doesn't fucking matter*.) It says that in order to be a successful dead person, you need to go beyond just throwing away the things that don't bring you pleasure, but to also consider the feelings your friends and family might have about those items.

The main question you're supposed to ask yourself: "Will anyone I know be happier if I save this?" This is another mantra that we don't need. Remember the indifference concept I taught you? Use it now. Relax. You've earned it. And you've earned all your glorious stuff. Now go watch some British television.

Quiz
when will you die?

1. When you watch TV you like to snack on:

    A. Green beans

    B. I don't watch TV, I prefer exercise

    C. Rosé

2. How many sexual partners have you had:

    A. 49

    B. Let me check my list. I have it framed in the bedroom.

    C. They are me and I am them. We are vast. We contain multitudes. The number is infinite.

3. What kind of unicorn are you?

    A. White horse, pink mane

    B. Silver horse, purple mane

    C. Stuffed

Answer Key:

Keep in mind this is a scientific quiz.

Mostly As: Sooner than you'd like.

Mostly Bs: Sooner than you'd like.

Mostly Cs: Nice work. You're immortal.

The FIB method of satisficiency and the art of doing just enough has the power to change your life

Obviously your life is still the same and books don't change anything (unless you read Ayn Rand's *The Fountainhead* when you were sixteen and now go around talking about how down-on-their-luck people just need to pull themselves up by their bootstraps. I know a wealthy dude who never gives money to a homeless person in case they use it for drugs instead of food. This is the same kind of person who argues against safe injection sites and doesn't want homeless shelters or low-income housing next to his condo building). But hopefully you've now got a bit of perspective about how our bullshit quest for success is making us miserable. You now understand the science behind why doing less is actually more. It's a relief, isn't it? To know that working out less and laughing more is better for you. To know that quitting your job and taking another one can actually make you more money. To know that washing an apple with just water rather than expensive fruit soap won't kill you. There are probably better takeaways from the book than the ones I just listed. But what the hell. I've probably written just enough.

acknowledgments

Many thanks to my brilliant editor, Ann Treistman, who has the best ideas and most of the talent in our partnership. And many thanks to everyone at The Countryman Press and W. W. Norton.